LIFE ON MARS: THE REAL STORY

by Johanna Biviano
Illustrated by Eric Reese

PEARSON

Scott
Foresman

Editorial Offices: Glenview, Illinois • Parsippany, New Jersey • New York, New York
Sales Offices: Needham, Massachusetts • Duluth, Georgia • Glenview, Illinois
Coppell, Texas • Ontario, California • Mesa, Arizona

Every effort has been made to secure permission and provide appropriate credit for photographic material. The publisher deeply regrets any omission and pledges to correct errors called to its attention in subsequent editions.

Unless otherwise acknowledged, all photographs are the property of Scott Foresman, a division of Pearson Education.

Photo locators denoted as follows: Top (T), Center (C), Bottom (B), Left (L), Right (R), Background (Bkgd)

Opener: Corbis; 1 ©Forrest J. Ackerman Collection/Corbis; 4 Eric Reese; 6 Eric Reese; 8 ©Reuters/Corbis; 12 Eric Reese; 15 Eric Reese; 17 ©James Marshall/Corbis; 18 Eric Reese; 20 ©Forrest J. Ackerman Collection/Corbis

ISBN: 0-328-13486-4

12 13 V0N4 13 12 11 10

CONTENTS

Chapter 1
Blast Off to Mars!

I ran as fast as I could, without stopping to catch my breath. My heart was pounding. There was a Martian running after me—huge and green and slimy, with six tentacles, three eyes, and a big blue mouth! Could I outrun it?

Then I felt it. Something wet wrapped itself around my ankle. I staggered and fell, incapable of further movement. But I wasn't incapable of summoning up a scream.

"Don't eat me!" I shouted loudly.

Then, to my horror, the Martian loomed near and grabbed me by the shoulders with one of its big tentacles. I screamed again. "No! Leave me alone!"

To my surprise, it screamed back.

"Wake up, Lisa! Wake up, honey, it's just a dream! Open your eyes now," said Dad.

I rubbed my eyes. "I dreamed a Martian grabbed my ankle. It was going to eat me!"

Dad hugged me. Our dog, Hubert, leaped up on the bed and licked my face. "Lisa, you're watching too many scary movies," Dad said. "If there were huge carnivorous Martians, we would know about them. And I know for a fact that there are no Martians in our house!"

"Okay, Dad," I said. "But can Hubert sleep on my bed tonight?"

Dad laughed. "Sure he can. Now get some sleep."

The next morning at breakfast, my mom said, "Your father tells me you've been dreaming about Martians again."

"One Martian," I said. "He was invading Earth."

My mom smiled. "There's a better chance of our invading Mars. In fact, we already have, in a manner of speaking."

"How did we do that?" I asked, puzzled.

"Well, NASA, the government agency that runs our space program, has sent these robots called rovers to Mars. Rovers are small, wheeled vehicles that are loaded with cameras and various kinds of sensing devices and can gather all sorts of information to transmit electronically back to Earth."

"Did the rovers find Martians?" I asked.

My mom gave me a hug. "They haven't found evidence of any life at all. At least not yet," she said.

I thought about Mars on my walk to school. My friend Jim caught up with me.

"Hey, Jim," I said, "did you know that the United States is exploring Mars?"

"Oh yeah? Well, what if the Martians don't want Mars to be explored?" Jim asked.

"Jim, there aren't any Martians," I said doubtfully. "Or at least there's no evidence of any."

"How do you know for sure? Maybe Martians are invisible," Jim said. "Let's ask our science teacher, Mr. Teschi. He knows everything."

A Mars exploration rover

That morning in science class, we queried Mr. Teschi about life on Mars.

"No one knows for sure," he said. "Why don't you two find out more about Mars for a science project?" That was something I was suddenly excited to do! I looked expectantly at Jim.

"Blast off to Mars!" Jim said.

Chapter 2
Being There

At the library, Jim and I got stacks of books about Mars, and as we read them, we learned so many new and fascinating things!

That night, when I fell asleep, I dreamed I was on Mars with Jim! I had read that humans couldn't breathe the thin air and that Mars was $-82°F$, which was *way* below freezing. But in my dream, we were warm and breathing easily. We were riding an exploration rover too! "I feel so light," I said.

Jim told me that was because there was less gravity on Mars. "In fact," he continued, "The gravity on Mars is only abut 38 percent of gravity on Earth, so if you weighed 70 pounds on Earth, you'd weigh—um—"

"Never mind," I said. "You'd be even lighter. You'd still be the runt!"

I know all sorts of impossible things can happen in a dream. And this was one dream from which I didn't want to wake up.

Jim and I trudged across the dusty soil. Mars was so different from Earth! Without any oceans, trees, or plants, it looked like one big desert. Just then, we came to a huge series of canyons, rilles, and trenches.

"I read about this!" I said excitedly. "This is the Valles Marineres. And it's 2,500 miles long! That's as big as the whole United States!"

Just then, I heard a rumbling sound. "What was that?" I asked, feeling just a little apprehensive in spite of myself. "It's not a—Martian?"

Jim looked scared too. The sound grew louder and louder. Suddenly, we saw what was making that peculiar rumbling noise. Two exploration rovers were lumbering toward us. We could see their names printed along their sides: *Spirit* and *Opportunity.* Those were the same two rovers that had landed on Mars on January 4, 2003! Here they still were, collecting soil samples and taking pictures.

"Let's go this way," Jim said. "I see something over there."

We came to an area that looked like a dried stream. "There are supposed to be big sheets of ice underneath the surface of Mars," Jim said. "Do you think there could be something living in the ice? Like Martians?"

"Wait," I said. "Back on Earth, scientists have found microscopic organisms that don't need the sun's energy to survive. They can be as deep as 3,300 feet below the surface, hibernating inside layers of frozen ice and soil. If they're thawed, these organisms come back to life! Could Mars have this kind of life?"

"It could if Mars had water! " Jim said excitedly.

Both of us stared at the dried stream bed. Living things had been found in freezing temperatures on Earth; maybe they would also be found here! I wasn't thinking about slimy Martians anymore—I was thinking of tiny life forms. And this time, I wished I could see them!

I was hungry, but nothing was growing on Mars, and there sure weren't any supermarkets or convenience stores around. "Here," Jim said. He took a big chunk of chocolate out of his pocket and handed me half.

"Where did that come from?" I asked. Jim told me to remember that this was a dream. Anything could happen.

I looked at the sky. I was lonely for Earth. "How would we even know life if we found it?" I asked Jim. "What should we be looking for?"

"All life forms that we know of have carbon," Jim said. "Maybe we can find fossils. They would tell us if there was life here a long time ago." He looked down at Mars's surface. "I don't see any fossils, though, do you?" He was very disappointed, and so was I.

"If Mars doesn't have life, why do we care about it?" I asked.

Jim looked thoughtful. "Well, if Earth becomes too polluted, we might want to have the option of living on another planet."

"That's true," I said. "And if we could figure out how to live here, we could learn more about Mars firsthand. We wouldn't have to rely on a rover. We could learn about how life begins on a planet, and whether there could be life on other planets."

Suddenly, everything on Mars was getting hazy. "Lisa!" I heard, and the voice sounded familiar. I shut my eyes for a second, and when I opened them again, I was in my bed on planet Earth! My parents were in my room.

"I dreamed I was on Mars again!" I said. "But this time it was great!"

I couldn't wait to get to school. As soon as I saw Jim, I told him about my dream. I thought Jim might laugh at me, but instead he nodded. "Someday, maybe we will get to Mars," he told me. "I wish I had had that dream too!"

"Well, you were in it!" I told him.

Chapter 3
How to Live in Space

All that week we worked on our report about Mars. We couldn't wait to give our talk in front of the whole science class! And the funny thing that happened was that the more I learned about Mars, the more my image of a slimy green Martian started to fade.

When I told my mom this, she smiled. "When you're afraid of something, sometimes the best thing to do is to learn all you can about it," she said. "I'm proud of you."

At last, the day came for Jim and me to give our report. We told all the kids everything we knew about Mars. All the kids had questions, but finally Mr. Teschi said, "You two have done an amazing job!"

Mr. Teschi told us that scientists were working hard to make it possible for humans to live on Mars. They were even trying to grow plants in space! Imagine trying to water a plant in zero gravity, when what the water wanted to do was bead up and float around!

Then Mr. Teschi told us about Biosphere 2, a huge system of indoor environments sealed off from the outside world. Eight people had lived inside it for two years to learn how humans could survive without any help from the outside.

"Do you think the Biosphere is proof that we can survive on a planet like Mars?" Mr. Teschi asked the class.

"I don't know," said Jim thoughtfully. "Mars has a lot of radiation in its soil. Could a Biosphere keep that out?"

"We don't know that, yet," Mr. Teschi said.

"Furthermore, Biosphere 2 was on Earth," I said, "where all the plants grew in normal gravity. We don't know if a Biosphere would work on Mars. At least not yet."

Everyone in the class got a little quiet. I think we all wanted to believe it just might be possible to someday live and work on a place as cool as Mars.

Biosphere 2

Chapter 4
The Next Martians

That night, my dad took out our telescope and pointed it at the sky. "We can't see Mars right now, but it's up there," he told me with a grin.

I looked up at all the stars, trying to imagine whether there was life on any of them.

"You know, I read that there was a meteor from Mars that fell to Earth," Dad said. "It had tiny little organisms in it, smaller than a human hair. They looked like bacteria, and they were more than a billion years old!"

"So that shows that life did exist on Mars once?" I asked excitedly.

Dad nodded. "We think it does," he told me. I was amazed.

We looked through the telescope some more, and then Dad and I went inside the house. Dad made hot chocolate. "You know what, Dad?" I said. "I'm not afraid of slimy green Martians anymore."

"That's good, Lisa!" Dad said. "Maybe someday you'll get to Mars for real."

"I hope so!" I said. "And you know what? I think that the next Martians anyone sees won't be slimy or green or anything nasty. They'll be humans living and working on Mars! *We'll* be the Martians!"

Mars in Popular Culture

Everyone seems to love the idea of Martians! You can find them in books, movies, TV programs, and on the radio. In 1938, on Halloween night, Orson Wells broadcast a radio play, "The War of the Worlds," in which he pretended to broadcast a real Martian invasion. Thousands of people panicked and fled for their lives!

In the 1960s, there was a TV comedy called "My Favorite Martian." This show was about a human-looking Martian whose spaceship crashed on Earth. He befriends a man who hides him while he makes repairs on his ship. The Martian even had little antennas on his head!

Martians have attacked people in dozens of films! These movies have thrilled audiences with special effects and frightening aliens, and some, like "Mars Attacks" and "Abbott and Costello Go to Mars," have made audiences laugh.

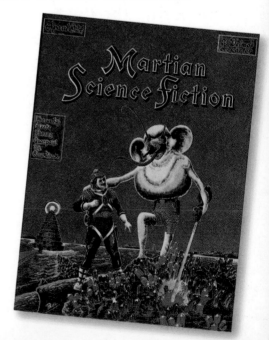